George Hansen

What is a Kindergarten?

George Hansen

What is a Kindergarten?

ISBN/EAN: 9783743318137

Manufactured in Europe, USA, Canada, Australia, Japa

Cover: Foto ©Thomas Meinert / pixelio.de

Manufactured and distributed by brebook publishing software
(www.brebook.com)

George Hansen

What is a Kindergarten?

"Close the lid of the trunk and strap the satchels. Let us turn the back to the city and run for the country where dear grandfather expects his flock for the holidays !"

The last railroad station is behind us, and, through fields of waving grain whence larks rise to the clouds to praise the glorious summer, the way leads to the village where grandfather reigns over the diocese of Jeinsen and its tributary ecclesiastics.

Here is my kindergarten. Acres upon acres, with houses and barns, with a walnut tree overshading the home of dozens of rooms, with wasps in knot-holes, with meadows on slopes to willowy brook, with cows and horses, with chickens and haystacks, and, be sure to note such, the old family coach in the shed.

And here is my kindergartner.

Behold the venerable figure as it passes along the lanes greeted with bow and lift of cap by old and young alike. His office, with piles of papers with foreign stamps, and with instruments of all descriptions, was a veritable museum to us. It never needed a bell to call us to the daily lessons. We were there upon the minute to listen, now to a talk on the wonders of the waterdrop, then to the descriptions of

3

barbaric tribes in far away Isles. Oh, let me dwell upon that important day when I received my first lesson in grafting trees! I think of him now as a saint as he knelt on his crutched cane and helped me splice the scion and the stock. I trust the day may come when I may pilgrim with our son to that spot, as I do now in fond imagination!

As I listen to the happy prattle of the child at my knees, and, looking into its eyes see the same brightness and color as the eyes of my kindergartner, why should I believe that the simple sandstone monument near the bleak commons of far-away Herzberg-am-Harz marks the spot where all that I embraced of him rests for ever? And my kindergarten, do I not see it now — this very minute! I walk up to the portal and find him seated on the green garden-bench as of old. The large rosebed spreads out before him, with the Kaiser von Marocco, the Duke of Edinburgh, the Maréchal Niel, the Souvenir de la Malmaison, all those sturdy old-timers which we budded to the twigs of the standards. There he sits, the wide screening cap drawn over his face to protect the eyes from the glaring sun. And the thoughts which go through his mind as he sits there on the evening of his life? Oh, reader mine, I have looked into his eyes so many times that I trust — at last — I have caught these threads of thoughts and woven them in new ply and new woofs. Here they are, covered by the lid which reads:

What is a kindergarten?

4

CONTENTS.

INTRODUCTION.

A kindergarten—a children's garden. We have accepted the term for our language, but have not absorbed its fullest meaning. With this I do not say that Frœbel, the most fundamental of all reformers, understood a kindergarten to consist of walks and lawn and plants with happy children as the fortunate possessors. I mean more. The writer of these paragraphs, who never attended an established kindergarten and yet enjoyed the kindergarten in its most unrestricted meaning, who developed in a profession on just such lines as Frœbel laid down, feels it his duty to build upon and build out Frœbel's lines with the aid of his professionalism. I have in mind a kindergarten which has added to all of Frœbel's methods the fullest complement which nature can place within a child's reach and comprehension.

This land of vast dimensions must do more than merely accept Frœbel's teachings. We must improve upon them, and bestow upon them that liberality which is ours, as soon as an occasion appeals to us. The time is drawing close when the kindergartens will be made part of our free school system. How will we be prepared for such change? Shall we move from the empty stores and vacant flats, now set aside for our children, to the basements of the school buildings? Let us give the matter our most earnest study, and let us realize that it is easier to direct the run of a brooklet than to change the volume of a deeply bedded river. The broad acres of our United States are yet comparatively undivided, and, except where the most expensive real estate demands business buildings to tower skyward, none are too costly to furnish the ground upon which our kindergartens shall be founded. Let us insist at the very outset of our movement upon the proper reservation, and nothing will prevent us from securing for our children what, through them, will redound to far more benefit to the land than the most gorgeous improvement we could devise.

The kindergarten as I design it is not an ideal. It is a composition of everyday facts, the attainment of which is a matter of principle, not of effort. One hundred foot frontage of a lot of average depth is the proper size for our grounds, whether such be a part of some school grounds or laid out by itself. Every other lot of less acreage is a makeshift. Our improvement must impress as a home, and as such, requires neither a board fence nor a hedge as a barrier. The house should be of rural design, perhaps with wide eaves and shingled, or of plaster work. The ground floor should be taken up by the schoolrooms, and the upper story, or half story, by the living rooms of the kindergartner. Whoever is in charge of the premises has to make her home in them. Do not attempt to impress a child with the sanctity of home in spaces which chill from lack of a cheering voice. I speak of a woman when referring to the kindergartner. Children of the age of four to six years are to be associated here, and at that time they need a woman as caretaker. It needs her endless patience, her ever ready care to rear the child. On a one-hundred foot lot three class rooms can find accommodation and playgrounds. Aside from accustomed use our grounds can and should serve as day nursery for the neighborhood. There may not be a woman near who is forced to work out and leave, during such time, the care of her children to others, but many a mother would gladly embrace the opportunity to leave her little ones in such surroundings when duty calls her from home. The kindergartner requires assistance, and her associates, as they are trained for the work, are the proper ones to attend such cases during non-school hours.

I have nothing to suggest towards the teachings in the schoolroom. My purpose is to exemplify how our task of forming the child's mind can be rendered easier and more correct. I want to do such through the agency of outdoor exercise amongst plants and flowers, and I give a list of those which are the most important, mentioning also some which are to be avoided. The connection between plant-life and human-life is fully as intimate as people demonstrate every day. It is for a good reason that at the birthday of friends we express our wishes through flowers. We know that our sympathy for the bedridden is more tenderly worded through the language of blossoms. And when the end has come to those dear to us, we bedeck them with the choicest flowers we are able to procure from garden and field. We compare a man to an oak, a woman to a birch, a girl to a lily, a boy to a weed. This surely has foundation in reason. Yet, the teacher shall not attempt to explain any of the habits of those plants with which I insist the child should be surrounded. Some of those habits are not yet understood; others are ·not comprehensible for a child;

and those which are evident in their natural simplicity will reveal themselves to the child in due season. Remember, every child in your charge is an Edison, every tot a Columbus, and the idealizing disposition of all of them sees a Garden of Eden in a vacant lot. I insist upon mere association of plants and children. Even if the habits of the former are apparently overlooked by those less responsive to the development of bough and leaf, the fact of having been in such association will make itself manifest in after-years. Through the company of plants we add an element of attraction, and a stimulus for which nothing else can be substituted. We should carefully discriminate in what is to surround our children at this age. If we are successful in our attempts, we will be able to do away with the multitude of palatial reform schools and improvement leagues of all descript and nondescript. If a community would establish sufficient kindergartens of such type, it would require only one generation to remodel the morals of its population. We mold and reform in every direction, and maintain the most complicated machinery for the application of so-called justice; whereas, the mere investment in simple kindergartens would render unnecessary the endless ramifications of those institutions. The existence of jails and asylums is no credit to a nation. It is, in the first place, admission of the fact that the early life of its people has been neglected. Give me a nation whose youth is reared in kindergartens like mine, and a prophetic voice exclaims: "To forbid a citizen to re-enter his home for a period of years will be the worst punishment you could inflict upon a wrong-doer,"

THE
CHILDREN'S GARDEN.

COMPANIONSHIP OF PLANT AND MAN.

The division of the grounds is only a part of the designing of the landscape architect. Through it we are supposed to be placed in full possession of and communication with the attractions which the setting is to furnish. Yet, while the partition of the area admits of ready correction, as the foot will make the trail where its passage is justified, the setting, while finished, undergoes a constant development. The forms as molded are the embryo, as it were, and every season's growth brings out more clearly either the mistakes or the advantages of the artist's design. It is seldom that we see the value of the setting placed above and beyond the importance of the division, and for that very reason I take the pains to positively state that the value of my booklet is mainly in this part of the designing.

The principle upon which I found my doctrin is consistency of association. I am forbidden to apply such throughout the design of a kindergarten, because I have to select mainly with the idea of associating the child with the plants, not plants with plants and children. But even in this regard I have assumed responsibility, the justification of which the child will prove, if the grown man will remain incredulous. As soon as we set out a plant, we make it a prisoner. It may die of want of proper condition, as it is called, of home-sickness, as I dare put it. Remember, it is firmly bedded where men placed it, not in a position of its own choosing. Has it ever struck you why so many annuals have to be sown and re-sown only to disappear as the new season opens? You may offer dozens of reasons, all of which may prove correct. But let me add one, the importance of which has not appealed to everybody : the seed was sown where it could not naturalize. I will illustrate by a few instances why plant-life offers such attraction to the scientist and such infatuation to the poet.

The common dandelion has traced civilization wherever it penetrated unexplored regions. We call it a weed, scientists term it a cosmopolitan and permit it to upset all the rules of plant geography. May I put the question : why does this dandelion follow the step of man wherever he goes?

Along the path from my home to the village grow tufts and tufts of a plant very similar to dandelion (Agoseris). I leave my home at an hour when the sun has risen just above the tops of the pines and gum-trees overshadowing the path. Why is it these dandelions all look into my face at this morning hour? Is it because I stand with the rise of the sun and they have turned their golden faces to greet its glory? But more than that. Why is it that on cloudy days this sea of faces is gone, as it were, and I have to walk amongst them to be able to greet them?

Let me select another everyday companion of ours for illustration. Along the roadsides grows a flattened weed of unpretending appearance. It belongs to the buckwheat family (Polygonum aviculare) and is grayish-green as much in stem as in leaf. It bears insignificant blooms of whitish-pink close to the prostate stem. This plant becomes the more plentiful the more you approach human habitation and is in its glory if trampled under foot. More than that even, it will do best when in a dusty road where driven over, day after day, by wagon wheels. I recollect stopping over, the eve before I reached the Calaveras Grove of Big Trees in the Sierra Nevada range, in an offing along the roadside at an elevation of about 4,500 feet. Even if I had not found scantlings and pieces of boards along the gulch and tumbled down cabins under the shelter of trees, the lawn of this Polygonum weed, as it spread closely to the ground all over the knoll, would have told me that man had a place of abode at this spot. Further investigation did show even more. Here where people had left the range and no more teams traveled and no foot pressed down the sod, the plants were smaller and half erect. And as it is there, so it is near your front door. The further your Polygonum weed is removed from the roadside, the more erect it becomes, even if in a place entirely free from other herbs. And wherever you trace this weed in other positions where the surroundings may appear to be in contradiction to what I explain, show patience and await development. Remember, that unlike seasons produce varying results and that it is far different for a plant, especially a weed, to grow in a place, than to be naturalized in that particular spot.

These examples have presented relations of plants to human kind. I beg leave to illustrate an instance where insect-life is so intimately connected with plant-life that its mere mentioning will justify the stress I lay upon association. Over the swamps of Madagascar, attached to trees, dangle the air-roots of a gigantic orchid, Angræcum sesquipedale. Sideways to the flattened growth of stem and leaf stand the spikes adorned with large shining stars of ebony flowers. The odor of this bloom is noticeable in day-time and strong when night sets in. Truly, nothing could prove plainer that there is a relationship between the odor and the insect which is about in those regions at eventide only.

But let us follow this plant and insect. The monstrous nightmoth has to rest upon the labellum of the starry flower to unroll its long proboscis and reach down to the store of nectar accumulated for its attraction in a spur of ten inches and more. The sexual organs of this orchid are so constructed that only cross-fertilization will satisfy its requirements. Many orchids assume a rigidity after such act has been performed, others wilt and hang lifeless over the vital organs. This orchid belongs to the former class, and to further protect the spot where its life has reached the summit of development, it folds the side wings over that place for protection against further disturbances from unsought visitors.

I offer no explanation for this fact, nor have I answered any of the previously put questions. I mention them to prove the existence of relationship far deeper founded than the general observer ever dreams of. I recite them as an introduction to my list of plants for the kindergarten and I will not attempt more than to suggest points of interest for the child in the plants selected.

Later on I give two illustrations how these kindergartens could be planted, mention plants which are suitable, and point out some which should be avoided. For any one to plant promiscuously any or all of the species mentioned in any kindergarten is as absurd as to take a certain number of any group and try to associate them with a fraction of the lists of another. Every single spot planted requires a setting of its own, dependent upon surroundings, upon exposure, upon local climate, upon the fancy of the designer, and is the work of a professional. My views are expressed in relation to temperate climes, and, while I indicate a few kinds which will prove too tender for some localities, there are plenty to select from for any requirement.

SIDEWALK TREES.

What the frame is to a picture, the sidewalk tree is to a house; both are needed. The Elm should be avoided. Its flowers count for little and its dimensions forbid setting on a small thoroughfare. The Horse-chestnut is excellent for wide avenues but will not succeed in warm climates where smaller growing Buckeyes should take their place. Maples are good and offer additional attraction in their seeds which are ever welcome to the varied purposes the child will find for them in its play. But the streets should be at least eighty feet wide for a Maple. Tuliptrees are acceptable in warm climates; in cooler ones they outgrow their space. Mulberries are good everywhere, in dry positions as well as in moist. So is the Birch, and very attractive to the child and deeply impressive through its graceful character. Its pendulous limbs suggest lightness and airiness. The bark offers many interesting ideas, and a little scribbling on its paper surface is treasured highly. The Aspen, full-brother to the Birch, is decidedly to be avoided. It is irritating to grown persons, and for a child to be forced to see it, and ever again see it, is absolutely criminal. Poplars are satisfied to stand in dry or wet soil, and while their dimensions are needful of large space, they will do well for a long time in even narrow streets, as they permit of great abuse. But they should be as far as possible from plantations, partly on account of the suckers which they send out, partly because they harbor a large number of insect pests. Alders will do best in wet spots, but are satisfactory also in dry places. Their many charms consist in the catkins, earliest of any in the season, and the burrs later. Their rigid growth is an objection of little weight. All Locusts are good, the pink one especially offers a beautiful green and an attractive blossom. The commonest will do well in the most disadvantageous positions. The Hawthorns are much to be preferred, and, with a little judicious thinning, will never assume the unclean appearance which they have in warm climates. Their flowers are rich hunting grounds for bees, and their berries are delightful to every child. The Mountain Ash, as well as the Oak-leaved Ash, are trees which we neglect too much altogether. It is surprising how well this tree of northern climes will do in warm zones. Its regular crop of bright berries is attractive to old and young alike. The Maidenhair Tree (Gingko) is proper yet rather too foreign for a child. Larch and Bald Cypress (Taxodium) will do in some exceptional cases. Acacias should be avoided inside the grounds on account of the rapid growth and the dimensions which they assume. They are good sidewalk trees in warm regions, their odor adding to the attractiveness of their graceful flowers.

The limited space of our grounds forbids the setting out of trees. We must resort to large shrubs for the elevated lines. Amongst them are the

FRUIT-BEARING SHRUBS. -

of first importance, the more so, as all of them also display attractive blossoms.

A Crab-apple is a child's delight. In bloom and downy foliage before any other variety, it is richly hung with blossom and develops a sure crop of fruit. Of the many varieties those with painted cheeks are preferable. Compare the amount of pleasure to be derived from such a tree with the limited charms of a large fruited apple, like the Alexander, or the massiveness of a Pound Pear. The boys are sure to fight over the yet green fruit of the Alexander, whereas the Crab furnishes fruit for the entire school. Plums are also welcome ; the Japanese varieties always produce fruit, which is acceptable and early as well, as are also some varieties of Cherry, Plum and Gages. The Damson is a bush which should not be missed. Its astringent fruit is a boy's delight, and the amount of temptation to impose upon the palate of fellow playmates or acquaintances is great and permissible. Quinces are very good. Their peculiar foliage, their very large bloom and, later, the fruit with its unsurpassable odor are attractive in every phase of development. To store away the fruit for months and let the children enjoy its perfume at Christmas is much appreciated by them. I refer also to Flowering Quinces. The many varieties of vari-colored blossom are charming to a child. This is the more conspicuous as the blossom is developed so very early in the season. If space should forbid the free planting of such a shrub, it can be trained against a wall and spread fan-shaped. As our kindergartens are apt to be caged in amongst higher buildings, this mode of training espalier should be adopted for many shrubs. Every one thus trained will be far more attractive in its way than massive vines which render a place chilly and require more attention. The Medlar is also a good tree, but of secondary importance only. The Persimmon is excellent. It reminds one of an Orange and will impress a child for the rest of its life through the strange development of foliage and fruit, a fruit as odd as it is glorious in appearance. The Hazelbush should be in every yard, and, while the green foliaged kinds of any Filbert Nut are pleasing, the purple variety is better, as it introduces a shade of coloring which no other shrub in our selection possesses. What child would not delight in the slender catkins, little streamers hanging from the branches, sending forth their showers of pollen dust in due time ? And then the nut hidden in its cap of frills and tucks ! How much more alluring than the naked nut from the grocer's sack are these nuts, especially when dots for eyes and mouth are added and a whole little face tucked within this natural bonnet.

Of bushes of less dimensions than those enumerated which bear also attractive fruit-stands, I mention the following. Brier Roses are pleasing through their bloom, their bright colored hips and also·through their delightful odor. Rosa pomifera should be resurrected from its forgottenness and be set out oftener even than the Japanese Rosa rugosa. Purple Fringe, or Smoke Tree, is attractive through its strangeness in foliage as well as in fruit-stand, yet a child will always be unconsciously impressed as if those were a foreign element in its garden. Spindle-tree might well be set out, though of secondary importance. Snowberries are very acceptable, the more so as they fill in spaces and corners, shady and forbidding, where hardly any other shrub will succeed.

In the golden leaved Elder we have the best opportunity of introducing a color of foliage which is permissible with this variety. It forms a bright object and, aside from the fruit of the bush, the pith of the boughs offers material for many pretty toys. Staphylea might be mentioned as of secondary value.

In the so-called Duck-plant and in Colutea we have some of the most enticing objects a kindergarten should possess. The former (Sutherlandia) will do well only in warm climes, and in cold regions should be planted out under glass in all of those places where a greenhouse can be added. Its hollow fruit-bags assume the shape of a veritable duck, bill and tail and all, and set upon a dish with water, a child will find a toy which will keep it busy for many moments, if not hours. Colutea is a poor substitute for this attraction, but will do well outdoors in any climate. Its inflated fruit-bag can be made to burst with a loud report.

FLOWERING SHRUBS.

The bloom of early spring is the most attractive bit of life with which we can brighten a child's days. The awakening of nature is eagerly watched for by young and old, and the earliest blossom is the dearest of any. If there be no other space to set out in green or color, the assembly of the Peach or Almond, the Lilac or Laburnum, the Cherry or Plum, and the Pussy-willow should always be found with the children. To them might be added the Snowball, and of Currants, the golden or the purple. The Weigelia and Deutzia are of minor importance. So is also the Forsythia, though its golden shower of bloom before the foliage appears renders it an attractive object, suggesting its Chinese origin without offensiveness. A Cornelian Cherry (Cornus Mas) will find room where high shrubs are called for and where little light and attention can be given to them. I mention Chimonanthus, Halesia, Xanthoceras and Exochorda, as beautiful and good, also Calycanthus, the Soap Shrub, and the Mock Orange, Philadelphus. The Spiræas and Brooms lead the way into warmer days, and there is so great a number of them that their selection must be left to the detail work of designing any single kindergarten. The Tamarix, the rival of the Heather, is the daintiest flowering shrub for summer days and is very modest in expectation as to soil and care. Heathers are very charming for kindergartens. Diosma, Breath of Heaven, is a very good shrub in warm countries, and its sweet-scented foliage does not indicate that the roughest exposure will be gladly accepted by the plant.

Shrubs with sub-tropical appearance are not needed to complete a kindergarten, yet, I mention those which permit of use and are attractive to the child. All dwarf Magnolias are objects of admiration for the young, especially the M. Soulangeana. An Aralia, be it A. spinosa or Japonica, is a wonder in itself as it spreads out its umbrella-shaped foliage with thin flower-stands in their midst. Catalpa and Paulownia are very noble trees but should be near the property-line or be put out as sidewalk trees.

Shrubs with spines and thorns are to be established only where no injury can happen to the child. The Holly is dear to many and will fulfill the greatest of expectation. Where its spines are feared, put out some of the evergreen Barberries, or perhaps a few of the thorny Hawthorns, which, as well as the Barberries, furnish very bright stands of fruit.

We should not leave the trees and shrubs without mentioning a few which can find worthy application under exceptional conditions. I have in mind the weeping varieties of trees, like Ash, Willow, Caragana, Cherry, Elm and Mulberry, any one of which might be used to shape the arbor at the entrance to our grounds. Also, two coniferous trees.

Of these a Christmas Spruce should have a free stand, though it would there assume dimensions which we cannot forever set aside in our space. But there is no need to retain such Spruce after it reaches a height of fifteen feet when it should be replaced by a young one. For the children to be able to decorate some kind of a Christmas tree in their own grounds is a delight with charms entirely its own. I mention here that these Spruces will suffer a great deal of abusive treatment, and, if space should not permit a better place, they may be planted where they will develop rather one-sided. The other coniferous tree is the Larch. We have to select far more deciduous plants than evergreen ones, partly because the latter would render the grounds too damp, partly on account of the charms with which the deciduous shrubs surprise us when nature again dons its green dress. And at that very time the Larch is the brightest green shade tree we have. In the midst of winter its slender branches are as attractive as a string of beads. And these purplish cones forming already on young specimens, — is a baby's ear shaped more daintily?

Ere I pass on to other plants of woody growth, I have to mention a list of those offering characters which are either meaningless to a child, or of such strange expression that, for such reason only, the child will pay attention to them.

Foremost amongst them are the Fuchsias and the Lobster Claw (Clianthus and Erythrina). A child will make free to some extent with the former for the simple reason that it meets with those blooms wherever it beholds a garden. But there is chill about the flower which forbids the child to show affection toward it. This is truer yet with the oddly-shaped Lobster Claws. The little ones may select them on account of their bright color, but the build of the blossom is foreign to its sympathies.

The Double Pæonies are meaningless to a child, while the single ones are good, but almost too large to be acceptable. The Hydrangeas, gorgeous as they are, mean very little to it. We may select a specimen of them to place as a show-piece near the door of our house; but the child will look at the plant only with astonishment. So with the Snowball whose lifeless colored leaflets lack even the character of stamens. It may be taken for granted that flowers which are not visited by insects are objects of no interest to a child.

The golden flowered Corchorus (Kerria) from China, the single as well as the double, are objects of curiosity, but we seek objects with which a child will make familiar. The same can be said about the Pomegranate with its shiny foliage and its gorgeous bloom. Abutilons are attractive enough, and the varieties of those many beautiful colorings from which we can select are tempting, but how much more charm does not a child derive from the Canterbury Bell?

To shrubs like Jasmine, Heliotrope, and Lemon Verbena the unaffected child remains indifferent, and their strong odors are no justification for associating their kind in our grounds.

VINES AND CLIMBERS.

The airy build of the trailing and climbing plants exerts a powerful influence over a child. It is true that all plants grow and show variation in height and vigor, but the additional equipment of tendrils and the winding character gives to the vines a heightened interest. The ascending of the Morning Glory, and the twisting of grasping leaves of the Clematis, do not need to be pointed out to the child. They speak for themselves. The care which these plants require in fastening their runners and rearranging what became twisted will appeal to a child as the address of friends. Let a child observe now and then how such care has to be applied, and the little girl will make it a sacred duty to look out for some certain vines, and thus be educated for life's earnest duties.

I want to speak a word of warning about the careless setting out of climbers. I mention here, as at several other points, that the appointment of any grounds is work for a professional, and to him should be left the perfect arrangement of vines in the limited grounds. In none of the areas I deal with is there room for a Passion Vine. Yet, if its most peculiar flowers are considered needful to fascinate a child's attention, plant it at the entrance or at the outside fence. The same should be said about Tacsonias, either of which kinds succeed only in warm climes. It is not at all unlikely that in climes where the Cobæa scandens will grow, such vine would be picked out first of any as the best to clothe a wall or fence. I emphasize that its rapidity of trailing is very entertaining, and that its mode of fastening is always plain to the investigating eye of a child. The flowers, also, are large and bold, and the changing from pale-green to purple is another feature to attract attention. But this vine should be grown only as an annual and never be permitted to chill or dirty any kindergarten with the enormity of its runners.

Aristolochia, the Dutchman's Pipe, this noble leafed vine with its odd flowers, as well as all Tecomas and Bignonias, might well be placed against the house. Plants which are trained as vines yet are only spreading, thin wooded bushes, should be omitted in preference to the many other shrubs we have to select from. In this class belong Tecoma Capensis, Plumbago, and the White Jasmine (J. officinale). Akebia quinata is so peculiar a vine, and its handsome foliage of such originality, that we should try to find a place for it where its evergreen character will not chill the spot, nor its spread interfere with the care which can be paid to it.

I do not believe in setting out any single one of our garden Roses. Yet, there are a few Climbing Roses which deserve a place. The single Cherokee is foremost amongst them. Wichuraiana Roses are also worthy of a place, but of others which display nothing but a mass of color at time of bloom, I must maintain that our space is too limited to waste it by permitting uncalled for gorgeousness. The Wistaria is a very noble climber, and the higher we train it the better will it succeed and the more will it absorb the children's attention. Of Honeysuckles the deciduous variety is the only one suitable. Its profusion of flowers, its overpowering odor and its handsome foliage, are the very characters which raised it to such importance in song and folk-lore. All Grapevines are desirable. Is the position advantageous enough to permit the setting out of fruit-bearing varieties, so much the better. These vines should train high around the windows of the upper story. The Wild Grapevine, Vitis riparia, is so sweet in odor that it deserves a spot where cultivated kinds will not thrive. Their relations, the Virginia Creeper, Ampelopsis quinquefolia, and the Boston Ivy, A. Veitchii, should be in every kindergarten. Both are handsome in foliage, both are glorious in the rich tints of autumn. And while the former has a depth of color which the latter does not display, the original way in which it attaches itself to the walls against which it is trained makes it an object which cannot be neglected. Our gardens are apt to face some building at one side or other. Against such this Boston Ivy should be planted to take care of itself. The higher area should be reserved for it exclusively, whereas in the lower, the climbing Ficus repens should find the spot which it will cover. It will succeed only in warmer climates, but there it forms a charming object because of its characteristic foliage, the mode in which this spreads out, and the unusual green which it shows, planted either in shade or in sunny exposure.

Is it necessary to speak at length about the merits of the Clematis, and is it possible to give either variety the preference, large or small flowering kinds ? All of them are grand for our purpose ; all of them appeal to the child and its fancies. The large flowering kinds have faces as bright as stars, as warm as flowers, and their thin wood permits of general and plentiful setting out. The small flowering kinds, with their bushes and bouquets like orange blossoms, are a wonderful sight. Again, they are deciduous and can be placed where thick shade is needed during summer-time and dryness during the cool part of the year. And as their handsome runners permit cutting back and trimming just as fancy dictates, the stands of fluffy seed in fall are again an attraction for the child, equaled only by the Smoketree. If we set out some Hop-roots, let us be careful lest we overstock the place with the runners which are extremely dangerous in their spreading habit. Yet, the vines climb with rapidity and should be set out where little else will succeed, and their handsome fruit-stands are again the furnisher of many pleasant moments for our little ones. Jasminum nudiflorum is a much neglected climber but a very welcome one for our purposes. Could you find a more pleasant duty than to point out to your children the first bloom after winter has lost its severity ? No leaf is about and the greenish wood is barely an indication of life. But those showers of yellow bells, as they hang all over the runners, will be remembered by the child for its future life.

Most of the annual vines should be given over to the toy-gardens of our little charges. Instance the Morning-glories. Could we add more description than their names indicate ? Let me say only that the teacher will find great pleasure and arouse renewed and lasting interest, if she will make selection of the different colors and distribute the seed accordingly. Let some tots also have mixed seed and let each imagine what its crop will be like.   Similar charm is offered by the Runners, the scarlet as well as the white. They have clear and solid colors and the crop of beans to be harvested from them is the delight of the children.   The little girl will find a meal to take to mother, while the boy may grow his supply of beans to trade for marbles when such pastime is in season.   Nasturtiums are good anywhere and at all times. Neglect the running kinds in preference to the dwarf ones and take advantage of the many varieties which our seed firms now place upon the market.   This vine more than any other invites the child's care to lay up seed for the coming season, and can we instil more noble ideas into its young mind than to encourage such traits in it?

Lophospermum scandens is a vine which will succeed in warm positions only, but there it is a revelation with its hundreds of flowers, each one of which, tucked away amongst woolly-fleeced foliage, likens a lion's throat.

Ere I close the list of climbers, I have to mention a trailer which is small as well as pretty. The Kenilworth Ivy (Linaria Cymbalaria), Mother of Thousands. It should be set out in many places, and as often as the rough boy may destroy what the careful sister has set out, this grateful vine will again produce results from the small piece the intruder may have spared.

Of fruit-bearing vines, the

BERRIES

form a group by themselves, and are to play an important part in our kindergarten setting. The berries should be so distributed that they can produce ample crops, and such kinds should be selected which will assure regular returns. Select proper positions and arrange your grounds that the toy-gardens receive their supply of berries in preference to fences and boundaries, so that the little ones may claim proprietary rights in the many vines. Select of Blackberries and their hybrids those which bear freely while not growing too rankly. Raspberries and Currants must be represented as well as a few bushes of Gooseberries.

THE PERENNIAL BORDER.

This must furnish us the greatest diversity of bloom with the least amount of caretaking. There is no need whatever for any spot to be without a plant, and the ground under trees and along shrubbery should be amply furnished with a selection of herbaceous plants. A climate like that we enjoy in California should produce flowers from the first of the year to the last of December, and our efforts should be directed mainly to selecting those which will impress the child as marking distinct periods. Again, we may associate similar growth and bloom and harmonizing color-shades, and yet have a wide selection. But I lay the greatest stress upon the avoidance of all those plants which mean no more to the child than a mass of color. Such effects confront us in every garden, and while people are justified in grouping and massing in places where home grounds have to rely upon a wealth of color, in our limited area there must be no plant which means color and color only. I have already objected to the Garden Roses and Hydrangeas and add now the great mass of Geraniums. Not one should be planted in our kindergartens unless it be a vari-colored foliaged one, varieties which usually lack in brightness of bloom. A bunch of flowers picked by the child as it passes along the beds — and, surely, we do not intend to punish our charges for such! — should attract the eye less than the thought. Plants which produce a sudden burst of color are excepted from such iron-clad rule. To them belong, for instance, the Gladiolus and Flags. Either of them is a stately plant and the glow of the coloring of the former specially gives the child a surprise which we cannot equal with other kinds.

The greatest importance is placed by me upon those flowers which have faces, as it were. A child well notices the difference such blossoms display when they are held one way or another. And if he does not, are we not to develop him through association of characters which will shapen his mind and ideas? It is in days of after-years that he recalls the impressions he now receives while under our care. What is not understood, or realized, for years and years, the mere fact that it exerted a silent influence bears results no matter how irresponsive the mind appeared to be at the time it was subjected to this association.

The Pansies take foremost rank amongst the flowers with faces. But a Pansy is not a Pansy by any means. It requires exactly as much care to raise a poor flower as the most noble of all, and it is our sacred duty that we raise nothing but the most perfect. The faces of Pansies are like those of humanity: all of them are interesting, and while some are so exceptionally attractive as to call for universal notice, others display but few qualities to redeem them from the commonplace. Moreover, there are worse than commonplace faces amongst the Pansies. Some are so utterly vulgar that their appearance in any place is to be avoided, more especially with us, who are to select the inviting, and pick from it the most appropriate only. Next to the Pansies come the handsome Violas, a strain so sweet and simple in their delicate tints that we may well place a large number of seedlings in care of our little gardeners. Then the single Violets. Perhaps some wonder that I ascribe a face to a Violet. But such it has, and its sincere features, its modest nobility, have won for it the admiration of poet and artist through all ages. Whenever you are in doubt how to fill a space here or there, put in a violet and remember that it flowers the better the oftener the little tots transplant it and the more bloom is picked off for bouquets.

Of other faced-flowers I mention the long list of all Pea-vines no matter of what description or sort. Be they Lathyrus, the Sweat Pea, or the grand spikes of the noble Lupines, they are all welcome in our garden.

Another large family is formed by the Snapdragons and honey-storing Sedges. I class here the so-called Lionsmouth, Antirrhinums and Linarias, as well as Pentstemons and Mimulus of all kinds and almost any color. Remember, also, the common wayside weed Dead Nettle, Lamium album and purpureum, as they grow along hedges and pathways in the old country. No bloom has a richer supply of honey, and what the bees do not take to satisfy their needs, the children will pluck and absorb.

Leonotus Leonurus is one of the most stately herbs we could set out, and their whirls on gigantic stems attract through their odd color and their odd build.

The glorious Foxgloves and the Monk's Hood (Aconite) have to be omitted on account of their poisonous qualities. The family of Larkspurs, so rich in blue or bright in scarlet (Delphinium nudicaule) should hang out their unusual colors in summertime when bloom begins to be scarce.

Let us make sure lest we forget the Bleeding Heart. This shrub has attracted attention and absorbed the interest of young and old ever since the day of its introduction. With this plant the child should learn to appreciate the individual flower, and desist from plucking the long spray. Such can be accomplished by inducing the child to discover all the interesting parts which compose this flower. Our wild species of less showy, yet very similar, build should find room somewhere. Their small rootstocks will produce an abundance of modest blooms in any out-of-the-way place we may assign to them.

The Cyclamens and Dodecatheons are a child's treasure wherever it meets with them. The very name given to the latter in the region about here, "Shooting Star" and "Johnny-jump-up," are so characteristic of a child's fancy that we may well know that in the early spring these flowers are picked by the children in great numbers.

For sake of comparison I mention the Pelargoniums, or Lady Washingtons, as they are called in some parts. They belong to the class of flowers with faces. But their features appear painted and the mass of color is so profusely displayed that every bloom loses its character as a flower. They must be avoided in our grounds. If the kindergartner's fancy takes more friendly to these flowers than mine does, let me ask her to set out those varieties only which show rich markings in deep contrast. I have in mind the deep-velvety maroon and red kinds which are sufficiently beautiful to redeem all of those vulgar magenta varieties which are so repulsively displayed in ever so many gardens. Our grounds are small and the number of plants from which we may select so great, that we can well afford to let the children get acquainted with the Pelargoniums in other gardens than their own.

All other flowers in our herbaceous border may be classed as mere ornaments, lacking personality. But the varieties from amongst them which deserve notice are legion, and it is difficult to enumerate the best only.

The Hellebore, or Christmas Rose, is really beautiful only where the snow covers the ground in winter, and while we may grow it to satisfaction, we must forego its dearest friendship if we can not show the children how this flower will come up through the snow.

Of Primroses we cannot have too many. Let us select those only which are clear in color (Polyanthus) and well defined in their marking. The old-fashioned, sweetscented Cowslip should be represented, and the Primula acaulis should be found in the toy-garden of every child. These plants are kind enough to withstand all abusive care our little ones may bestow upon them. Liverwort, Hepatica, and Lungwort, Pulmonaria, are other kind messengers of spring. Forget-me-nots should be everywhere and those varieties which require more watering should be handed over to the busy hands about the toy-gardens. Likewise, Daisies may be left to all the abuse the little gardeners will afflict. Repeated handling seems to be appreciated by them, and it will be the very plant which may be looked after every other week to see whether it is making roots.

Anemones in all their glory should furnish a great amount of variation in our border. While the herbaceous kinds flower late in summer, the bulbous varieties may readily be handed over to the little hands and a liberal supply be parceled out to the toy-gardens. They are the very flowers which will amply repay with bloom, and that of such a coloring as will swell the pride of the little nursery folks.

The perennials furnish us a choice variety for summer-flowering plants. All the Sunflowers and Black-eyed Susans are stately and well endowed with bloom. Marguerites flower all the year round. The colored Pyrethrums in their many pleasing shades bring about variety and charm. The Michelmas Daisies conclude the display of their kinds in fall. Some Dahlias, also, should be set out and the taking care through winter of their bulbs in cooler climes places further responsibility upon the little gardeners. The single blooms are the most appropriate in our gardens.

The herbaceous Spiræas and their relatives are all a sweet assembly and their graceful flowerstands are an attraction in any place. Spiræa filipendula is the queen of their kind and

S. Ulmaria the king. Gypsophila, Baby's Breath, is unique in its light, airy build.

The stately rows of Hollyhocks should find room where their majestic spires may display in the full sun, and both the single as well as the double are to be favored, giving the preference to the former. Perchance a Mullein should be thrown in to raise its golden bloom on velvety stalks. The rosette of foliage of the plant in the first year is an attraction in itself and arouses great expectation for the season to come. The Canterbury Bells are another biennial, and their chimes will be repeated from many a little one's lips as it adds the sound to the handsome bell. Phlox, Pride of the Meadow, with its handsome heads of flowers and the agreeable perfume, should replace the gaudy Hydrangeas in our kindergarten. Columbines in all varieties are welcome to ample space in our limited area, and the more they spread and reach out their handsome flowers in natural array, the more welcome they should be for our selection. The yellow, red and white varieties are the most suitable, and buff and misty colors should be avoided.

The Carnation family is an association from which we may take all those forms which remind us of the state they were in before cultivation and mast-culture distorted them. Hunt up the oldest single pink and the little carnation so sweet and so simple, with which every old-fashioned garden borders its beds. Refuse to plant a double carnation. Their association favors ideas and conceptions which we fall into only too quickly when we grow up. The more double a pink, the less it is a pink. The wild Dianthus and Lychnis, the

Red Robins and the Lychnis flos cuculi are good friends. So is Silene inflata, a plant which will be endeared to every child on account of the peculiarly inflated calyx.

Out of all the multitude of perennials which could be mentioned with perhaps just as much justification as those I have listed, there are two which I place last in the list and first in importance. The St. John's Wort, Hypericum, is the most interesting of all summer flowers. Their liberal display of stamens makes them at once the handsomest and most inviting of all blooms in color at that time of the year. They flower abundantly, need little care and their yellow is clear and rich. The other plant is the old, dear old Red Top Clover. The leaves are attractive as clover leaves are, and the stem builds itself firmly and stately, displaying the handsome flower to wind and weather, to sun and clouds. A bouquet in itself, every single bloom is a store of sweet honey. This every child knows, you never need draw its attention to it. And is there a more interesting, a more idyllic picture in nature than to see the bee climb from bloom to bloom, gently nodding to and fro, and spend time over the rich harvest it is reaping?

Amongst the clover sow a few seeds of Anthyllis Vulneraria and Ornithopus rativus, the Kidney Vetch and the Serradella.

BULBOUS PLANTS.

Does it need more than the mere mentioning of Snowdrop and Daffodil, Anemone and Crocus to call to mind the sweetest charms with which nature has endowed us? Flora has no other children alike beautiful, alike innocent, alike fleeting. They spring up like beloved children, grow sweet and charming and, as if they were too precious to be soiled through contact with the world, they pass to the homes whence they came. But with every new awakening of nature they return as dainty as ever, brightly arrayed in their heavenly robes of surpassing purity to renew their yet vivid impression from the season before. And are not these the flowers of the children? Why does a tot reach for the Snowdrop, why does it break the Fairy-maid, why is the Narcissus its companion, greeted as a friend as soon as beheld?

And if these are children of the spring-time which I have named, there are also grown up and developed members of the bulbous garden. Not all of them fade away like the Crocus, some ripen to womanhood and charm us as the seasons pass on. They are the Watsonias, the Gladiolus, the Tigridias, the Ixias, the Montbretias, and, grandest of all, the royal lineage of Lilies. Do not tell me they are too tender, too easily destroyed by a child's longing hands, so that they should be eliminated from our list. Emphatically no. The days have passed when we were satisfied to give our children the gutter and the sidewalk, the kindergarten without the garden. It is only a question of progress when we shall establish all through the land the kindergartens as I proclaim them, and in the most advanced of them, Lilies will array themselves to be loved and adored by those most fit to understand their heavenly build.

There is no Narcissus growing with flowers of average size which is not a suitable object for our selection. The small flowering Roman or Italian Hyacinths do well and increase in size and number rapidly. Crocus of all description are welcome to display their golden or silvery cloth in our beds. Lilies of the Valley, with the most delightful odor of any petal opening, the Amaryllis with their leafless stems, the Crown Imperials with their leafy build, and the Trilliums with their oddest association of foliage and flower,—every one of them is suited and should be considered. Also the Dog-tooth-violets (Erythroniums), the Winter Aconite (Eranthis) with its large golden cup, the Anemones in thousand-fold glory, the Ranunculus in almost all hues of the rainbow, the peculiar Salomon's Seal: indeed, it is difficult to limit the enumeration.

Of those flowering in later months, the Callas, Cyclamens, Watsonias, some Crocus, the Red-hot-poker plant (Tritoma) and especially the Tigridias are a noble lot of color and shape. The pretty Colchicums we will have to omit on account of the injurious sap, but the large variety of Oxalis shall safely furnish us with bloom and brightness.

THE TOY-GARDEN.

Each child should be induced to take interest in caring for a little garden patch of its own. My plans provide for them, and under the direction of the city-gardener and the supervision of the kindergartner they may cultivate and sow and reap to their hearts' content. While all take part in the plants on the entire grounds, here, in the toy-garden, every one is supposed to apply its own little doctrines to the patch set aside for it. Naturally, most of the plants will be annuals and from them we should select quick growing and, if possible, showy kinds. The old-fashioned Strawflowers, Everlastings, should receive a place of importance in this collection. The pretty Acroclinium, the bright Calliopsis, the true Cornflower, the modest Mignonette, the slender Linums, the dainty Gilias, the fleshy Portulaca, the august Poppies, the showy Clarkias, the stately Godetia, the pompous Asters, the diffident Love-in-the-mist, and the gorgeous, openfaced Sunflower: they are all grateful objects for a child's gardening.

I want to mention at this opportunity how attractive plants are to a child if their development offers special features which will be quickly noticed. Those which close their bloom every evening and again reopen in the morning are notable in this respect. The sweet Baby-blue-eyes (Nemophila) and the California Poppies (Eschscholtzia) belong to this class. It is not at all necessary that we draw the child's attention to these changing conditions. We will feel awkward enough by the time one or the other of our pupils notices such conditions and asks us why they take place. We intend to educate the children through association, and must refrain from spreading before them what little wisdom we older ones possess. That is the reason I do not propose planting such species as Touch-me-not (Impatiens), or the Mimosa.

THE VEGETABLE GARDEN.

It depends on the space at our disposal whether we can afford to endow each child with a little spot in which it may grow vegetables, or whether the kindergartner has to keep the different kinds of vegetables in distinct patches and let the children help to cultivate and harvest. Whichever way may have to be pursued, the growing of vegetables is of prime importance for the children under our charge. Let us recollect that every vacant lot in our cities could well be planted after the plans of Mayor Pingree, of Detroit, and here, in the kindergarten, is the place to begin the training of the future cultivators of such useful plots. Let us forbear, though, most carefully from trying to point to such work as being of any cash value. The children should not know the difference in price of one coin from the other while they are with us in these sacred grounds. But that spirit should be cultivated,—to grow something to receive returns. And these returns should become the child's property to do with as he or she likes. Do you doubt for a moment that the few potatoes will go into mother's kitchen? That the handful of beans must be cooked for father on the coming Sunday? And what mother could be so poor that she would not be willing to season those potatoes with the best of butter, the beans with the richest of flavors, and embrace that child of hers with the fondest embrace?

Almost all vegetables are suited for our garden. Potatoes, with proper selection of those ripening early, should be lined with rows of Horsebeans. Do not shrug the shoulder over their kind. There are thousands who appreciate them, and it is well that the edges of the patches should be turned into use with growth which will produce ere the main crop is ready. Radishes, Lettuce, Beets, Turnips, and Carrots all ripen easily and surely. Of Beans we have already runners planted as vines. Let us add Bush Beans, and teach the child how to pick them with the greatest of care, so that the crop will not be ruined after the first handling. Tomatoes may be set out after having been raised from seed under shelter. We also should have a few roots of Asparagus. It is a highly ornamental plant and the child should know how that vegetable is produced. Corn of the early kinds must find a place and kitchen herbs of all descriptions must have ample room. Imagine the pleasure of a child if it can supply the home regularly with all the Parsley for soup and dressing ! Also rows of Strawberries to pick and put between the smacking lips. They furnish a good way to train the child to arrest its longing hands and wait till the sun has ripened the berry, which, then, should be disposed of as the teacher decides.

VARIOUS PLANTS.

The grasses furnish unique effects and some of them should be used in our compositions. I have in mind the beautifully colored Ribbon-grass, the small-growing Bamboos, the Snakegrass (Briza), the variegated Reed (Arundo) and some small kinds of New Zealand Flax (Phormium). The Pampas-grass must be left out. It is of dimensions unsuited for our grounds and its foliage is too sharp to be placed in contact with the little hands we have to protect.

Of succulents we may put out some on the driest and hottest spot in our garden. Cactus with its dazzling flowers is well suited for show as well as to illustrate the peculiarities of its genus. Hen-and-Chickens (Sempervivums and Echeverias) should be set out in limited number. The children may be permitted to plant and replant them as often as they feel the necessity of doing so. They will outlive all the trials to which they are subjected.

A half-barrel with water plants could well be sunk into the ground. A small growing Water-lily and a few Water-hyacinths will make their home in its boundaries. A Parrotsfeather (Myriophyllum), will also live in such company and overreach the border in graceful runners.

As the space for a small rockery can not be spared, we should select just two or three large boulders, so large that the children cannot shake them in their place. Set close to them a few Primroses, a Kenilworth Ivy and a few Saxifragas as well as Stone Crop (Sedum). It will suggest impressions which will grow with the child as it develops under new surroundings. Also a Moneywort, Lysimachia, in a damper spot should spread its regularly set leaves and unfold its large, golden flowers.

Plants with large foliage are a thing of necessity with our limited landscape. They suggest nobility of character and the wide space to which they are entitled impresses the child with a certain admiration. The most desirable plants of this class are the Rhubarb and the Artichoke, both of which show very noble flowers in due season. Also some Elephant's Ears (Caladium) and the classic Acanthus; a Castor Bean plant and a few Cannas, carefully selected, should also be included. But let us take care lest we encourage an expanse of foliage which is as meaningless as the gorgeous coloring of some flowering plants. A Palm, stately and distant, is no friend within our walls. No bird would light on its fronds, even if they were covered with birdseed. How much less should a child be insulted with a character which is as foreign to it as an apple-blossom to the Malayan. It is neither costliness nor rarity which decides with us in our selection. No Dracæna, no Camelia is entitled to any consideration. The most humble blossom which furnishes food for the bee or invites the swift humming-bird to a meal is far more important in our grounds than the most favored leaf from under a tropical sun.

THE LAWN.

The small patches of lawn which are laid out in our grounds are to provide the groundwork of green so essential to a cheering landscape. If they were to be used by the children at all time and entirely at their will, they would deteriorate in short order. The kindergartner has to place some restriction upon the use of them, for useful they must remain, even if they require renewing once a year.

But I want to lay down a new rule for lawns in such places. In the first place use that kind of grass which proved to be the most resistant in your neighborhood, no matter whether such is considered the most fashionable or not. Let the lawn be green. In states like California I wish to see the White Clover brought to the front. It is idle for us to boast of blue-grass lawns when the keeping of them is the cause of more expense than the result justifies. Then again, the sheen of the blue-grass is less acceptable than the warm green of the cloverleaf. The blue-grass rejects the warmth through its glossy foliage. The white clover absorbs the warmth, as it were, and stores it in unlimited quantity. There is no period of the season in which it looks yellowish and neglected. Some people object to the white and fragrant blossoms. But just in them I appreciate a character which no grass possesses. In our case they will furnish a new attraction for the children and invite them to play upon the ground. In fact, I would sow some Dandelion and many Daisies in my kindergarten lawns. If any person is in doubt whether such is the right thing to do, let him watch the children. It is for them that we adjust our improvements and they are the judges and directors of our efforts.

OUR ZOOLOGICAL PARK.

It would be unnatural to try and separate our children from animal life. And what could be more harmonious than their association? We older folks feel at all times called upon to subject children to instruction if not to correction. The association of child and animal excludes such and makes the former the king of the company. A cat even, to strangers the most perverse of domestic animals, will permit a child to almost squeeze it in two. A dog is the companion and full-fledged brother of the boy and the guardian and playmate of the girl. Whoever has observed the companionship of a lamb and children will recollect how playful they were in a thousand pranks, never tiring the whole, long day. We, who are supposed to direct our children's ideas and lead their fancies, should select the proper companionship from amongst the animals. Let us then exclude entirely the dog from our grounds. Only too many of them are associated with our children in the streets, and no dog ever displayed the proper qualities of its kind when spoiled through contact with children. Neither has the cat any right to be with us. There is no child which does not enjoy its company at home or over at the neighbor's. But we have to install a lamb in our garden. Let it assume charge of the lawn-mowing and let it be fed regularly under the kindergartner's supervision. Let the children learn, in contact with all the animals which I mention, that it is unwise to feed them at all times of the day. The lamb may be led forth at certain hours and whichever little girl had her birthday last may have the privilege to decorate the lamb's neck with a new ribbon.

Rabbits may be hutched with the lamb. Both will be on the ground floor and both permit friendly association. Above them the squirrels shall have their housing, and their caging and nest-building shall be in full view of the children. Guinea pigs can well be omitted from our collection.

Of other animals let the following be represented. Gold-fish can be kept in a glass for years, and it is well for the children to be called in when the changing of the water takes place. A Turtle may be kept if the tub with water-plants is level with the ground. Lizards and Horned Toads should also be on hand. They do not require care nor feeding, and if only left alone will domesticate in a short time.

Before I speak a good word for the last named animal which I propose housing with us, the Toad, an animal despised wherever spoken of, let me mention some facts which are known to everybody but not realized in their meaning. They go to prove a companionship the extension of which we ought to cultivate with religiousness.

There actually are at this day of our civilization some animals which refuse to be scared when they behold us. I will mention a few well-known cases. The first is the Lady-bird. Whether it is that nobody harms the pretty insect, or whether it is that those who were harmed did not survive the ordeal to report to the others, it is a fact that they associate with us wherever found. They will walk back and forth on our hand and take wing whenever they choose, no matter how much you may finger around them. Of birds I know very little, being shortsighted and, therefore, denied the pleasure of having acquaintance with them. But I have experienced that flocks of Quail will come and live with us in the woods as soon as they have found out that we do not object to them. On an out-of-the-way place where I stayed for years no quail was ever shot at. Neither were they fed. In all of the surrounding country every little boy and every grown man carried a gun as often as time and fancy would permit, and even small birds fell their prey. This proves that the quail would live with us if we did not force it to leave us.

Behold, also, the Sea-gull as she sails the air and leisurely follows the boats, indifferent to the noisiest crowd which may man them. Call them scavengers of the waters, if you like, but do not deny them their elegance and their stoicism. Does it not look as if they would light on your hand if outstretched to welcome them? Their large and friendly eye is turned towards you and a grateful recognition is made in bow and flight for every particle thrown to them. I have never observed that anybody entertained an inclination to harm them,—and would they move if you forced them to?

And now the word for my friend, the toad. This philosopher will live at our front door half buried under the pot of our most cherished house-plant, the Diogenes of the amphibia. He will take care of his cave and love life like the happy artisan who sits at his steps and smokes a pipe in the fullest enjoyment of life. When the toad goes forth to hunt his living he picks up what annoys us and devours a great number of bothersome insects. I have made pets of toads for years and have fed them with bluebottles and bugs till they looked for their regular repast in regular places. Humanity with its vicious superstitions owes a great apology to this much abused animal, and it is for us to uproot the senseless persecution to which it has been exposed for ages past. Let us have a dozen toads in our kindergarten and let it be kept clean and neat through their habits of devouring the nasty worms and insects which accumulate, especially in a city lot. It is needless to state that the toad is anything but poisonous, and that it only needs our common sense to notice that he is colored in very harmonizing tints, and that his clear and bright pair of eyes are as pleasant to behold as those of a pet dog.

A large cage for birds should be set up in every kindergarten, and almost any bird is welcome to our care, provided his captivity is not apparent to the beholder. Birdfanciers may be able to properly extend my list of birds suitable for our purpose. I mention some and they will prove sufficient for almost all purposes. The Canary has been imbred and held captive for so many generations that its caging will be only natural. It should have an opportunity to nest and raise broods. Doves, with their affectionate cooing, shall be associated with us. They are of handsomely colored plumage and always the picture of neatness and gentleness. Last, but not least, let us have a few Bantams in our enclosures. If space forbid a separate housing, they may go in the stalls with the lamb and rabbits. Their tiny forms and independent demeanor suit well with our composition, and the children will appreciate their company.

The gathering of eggs should be left to children by turns, also the feeding and watering under proper directions. At time of brooding Bantams are rather more fickle than other fowl, though only hens with exceptional dispositions permit interfering with themselves and their flocks.

I wish to state distinctly that no parrot has any right to be within our grounds. Do not let us disturb the pleasant company we create with such rude intruders.

CARE OF PLANTS AND GROUNDS.

A city nursery will form part of every rightly composed community. It will be an adjunct to the park management of the larger municipalities and as such have charge of the sidewalk trees, boulevards, squares, playgrounds, and school-yards. The care of kindergarten grounds like these is the most simple thing for one trained for such work. A foreman of the city nursery should have charge of all kindergartens. He could attend to twelve in the week's time and all extra work as the annual cleaning and shaping would be performed by garden laborers under his supervision. The park nursery will provide all the material which is of the most simple and inexpensive kind. As often as a child has injured or destroyed any of our improvements, they are to be re-established and no other punishment than mere advice to be administered. Our improvements are for use, not for ornamentation alone, and those who take care of them are required to place the children in the fullest possession of them.

DESCRIPTION OF PLATES.

If a glance at the series of plates gives the impression that every one of them might as well be the appointment of an area surrounding a private home as that of a kindergarten, their objects are served. For that is the idea incorporated in my booklet, that the proper setting for a home erected in the very midst of a busy city should be accomplished. We build and lay out for a family, the only difference being that our family is rather numerous in the flock of children. Necessarily, the buildings have restricted dimensions and the area is divided into many playgrounds and runways, but, aside from that, no home-builder could suit the purpose of his family better than by adopting a plan on lines as here laid down. It is possible to develop a mind and neglect the bodily welfare of a child, but the reverse is not imaginable if grounds like ours furnish the field of exercise for the forming body.

In attempting to illustrate the proper planning of kindergarten-grounds, I naturally fell into systematic lines. Every one of the plans accompanying this book relates to grounds of a level, or nearly level, area. This is unfortunate and, yet, unavoidable, as I want to address the largest circle of interested people, not merely professionals. I distinctly state that any slope to our grounds should be welcomed, and that such may reach fifteen feet on a fifty-foot lot, or twenty-five feet on a one-hundred-foot lot. In such cases the designs should guarantee an absolute originality, and every value in light and shade, in slope and rise, be put to fullest use. Such appointments would then add further worth and attraction for the benefit of our charges. For as we leave the level land and flee to the mountains to spend our vacation, so will a child avoid the street and seek the gutter and the bank on the unimproved lot to enjoy its pastime.

Originality in the designs as fitted to level areas must consist in the advantage which has been gained by overcoming obstacles and hindrances previously existing. I give five illustrations for kindergarten-grounds on lots of one-hundred-foot frontage—assuming in every instance that different conditions as to exposure and limitations through neighboring buildings exist. No matter how many kindergarten-grounds may be established in any one community, no two of them should be identical in design.

As properly chosen school grounds are of such extreme rarity that it is impossible to refer to them, I have been forced to confine my plans to areas separated from grounds used by older school-children. I wish to state, though, that concentration of school grounds would result in greater benefits in so far as we secure territory which is more open and impresses as more noble in its setting. Communities are slow to set aside the necessary grounds for breathing spots in our crowded cities, yet if all schools were set in entire blocks, surrounded by useful and pleasant grounds, a great problem of our economical conditions would be solved.

For the sake of comparison, I assume that every lot as illustrated is of a depth of one hundred and thirty-five feet, which is about the average we meet with in the modern city.

KINDERGARTEN ON A TWENTY-FIVE-FOOT LOT.

If such area be on an inside lot, it should not be improved for our purposes. If owned by the school department, it should be utilized as an income-bearing investment for purposes for which it may be suitable. Plate number one shows the improvement of a corner lot of such dimensions and demonstrates that it is possible to get proportionate returns from it. The improvements must be limited to a house 14 by 50 feet, the necessary shelter—which may, at times, during pleasant weather, serve as an extra schoolroom—sandcourts, swings, and teeterboards. We find room for a spot of green and use the narrow strips along the property-line for toy-gardens. Playtoys, and other apparatus, as perhaps hammocks and the like, may find accommodation under the shelter.

KINDERGARTEN ON A FIFTY-FOOT LOT.

Here, as in the previous case, the lot should be on a corner. Light and air are essential to our purposes if satisfaction is to follow our efforts. I illustrate three cases, the designs of which are conditioned by the location of the house. Air-wells can easily give light to the building if it has to be placed as is illustrated on plate number two. The grounds are all in front of the house, and the setting is ideal. The little lawn is halved by a pathway to admit running about. Yet, the green swath will impress as a whole, no matter whence you look at it, as the pathway crosses your view instead of paralleling it. There is plenty of playground, the shelter serving as such as well as the area around the sandcourt, swings, and seesaws. On fifty-foot lots we find ourselves permitted to accommodate some of our animal friends, and place them where least interfering with the apparatus, so that the little sightseers will not be in danger of being injured while watching the animals. Many toy-gardens admit of a great variety of cultivation. One way of planting this area is described in a subsequent paragraph.

The other corner lot, plate number three, has its house removed to the middle of the area. The shelter is in the back so that cultivation and irrigation may be carried on where the soil is exposed. The lawn is an undivided oval of about 30 by 50 feet. The house, 18 by 50 feet with an L of 10 by 18 feet, admits of a very pretty design. It is natural that the housing for the animals should be kept in the rear as much as possible so as to avoid attracting the crowd on the outside. We must also try not to bring them in direct touch with the playground apparatus, as the sightseeing and games should be kept separated.

A look at the design for an inside fifty-foot lot, plate number four, shows at once the difficulty of putting such location to proper use. The neighboring houses are bound to crowd us, and if the shadow of a tall building or the influence of a cold north wall should over-awe our improvement, it may as well be given up. A potato which sprouted, deprived of its full dues of air and light, may develop foliage, but it will lack in tubers and flowers. Only then, when open grounds of liberal homes are at our right and left, should such ground as this be improved for a kindergarten. The house should then be placed forward, the playground and shelter be kept in the back part, and the growing and irrigating be done in front where the brightest light possible can be enjoyed.

KINDERGARTEN ON A ONE-HUN-DRED-FOOT LOT.

Grounds of such area are proper for a kindergarten. If larger they would form school grounds, if smaller they are only makeshifts. Our buildings can now stand unconnected, if so desired on account of the neighboring houses, and we still will have the necessary exposure. We are independent of the improvements of the adjoining properties, and no matter under what disadvantages we may find our holding, we can accommodate our needs.

The corner lots are, naturally, the more valuable, and I illustrate four instances. In the first, plate number five, the house is in the middle of the grounds. It is wise to so place it if the neighboring lots are open in their improvements and are not apt to be built upon with high structures. The house here is 23 by 44 feet with an addition of 25 by 30 feet. It offers ideal arrangement and permits separate entrances to the schoolrooms and to the living apartments. In grounds like these we also have two entrances from the streets, provided the neighborhood is such that we have not more than the usual intermeddling to guard against. The patches of lawn are thrown in front. This serves a twofold purpose: we secure more pleasing arrangement as seen from the street, and the playgrounds may be located more unobserved in the shelter of the building. The lawn is laid out in pieces to offer different grazing grounds for the lamb. The divers holdings give the children an opportunity to respect rights and to divide care. We have a commodious shelter, 25 by 42 feet, freely placed apparatus, various toy. gardens and runways galore. A may-pole is placed, and strips for toy-beds and vines are encircling the entire lot. It is indeed a paradise, the Garden of Eden realized.

The next illustration, plate number six, finds our building in the very rear. Neighboring structures with high walls conditioned such, and we spread our depth so as to fit snugly against it. The wide grounds are almost undivided and, for those who lay more stress upon a green lawn than upon separate gardens, this design must appeal with force. Shelter, toy-gardens, apparatus, and animals are arranged so as to divide the area as little as possible. While it is true that this partition gives the impression that a very large number of children can be accommodated, it must be remembered that here it is more difficult to keep the classes and games separate, as will be required at times.

The next illustration, plate number seven, offers the house

attached to one on the neighboring lot, selected thus because free circulation and light had to be made possible from the other directions. If the house, 32 by 60 feet, should be found in need of extension, its upper structure could well overlap part of the shelter and more space be given to the inhabitants. The shelter, animals, and apparatus are kept in the corner, because a second building abutted at the rear of that lot and we have to keep that part as dry as possible. Lawns, toy-gardens, and apparatus find their accommodation according to the room left. This is a convenient arrangement and a picturesque setting of such grounds. A suitable manner of planting these grounds is described in a subsequent paragraph.

Plate number eight deals with grounds which are harshly walled in by neighboring buildings. Good light comes only from the front and all the color of green and the desirable shrubbery is here located. The building, 28 by 60 feet with an L of 20 by 22 feet, abutts the adjoining building and springs well out into the grounds to benefit from fullest exposure. The low shelter is kept in the corner towards the street and the toy-garden against the property line where the reflex from the house on the next lot warms it. The animals occupy the corner; seesaws, swings, and sandcourts are before these plots. Perfect dryness and circulation of air is secured in this part of the walled-in grounds. Two large pieces of lawn fill the foreground and give a rich setting to the building as seen from the street.

The last design, plate number nine, shows an inside one-hundred-foot lot. We feel at once the necessity of reducing the area to be covered by the building and select a T-shaped ground plan for the house so as to secure the greatest possible surface for light and air. The rear has to be kept dry and, consequently, warm, and aside from the shelter for animals and apparatus, we feel the need of setting aside a wide strip to keep our building warm and free. Lawns and toy-gardens are arranged to be under the least disadvantage from the neighbors' improvements.

PLANTING OF A KINDERGARTEN ON A FIFTY-FOOT LOT.

The planting refers to the design illustrated on plate number two. The west and south sides are towards the street. Those species set in [ ] alongside the other enumerated kinds refer to plants which can be substituted in climates warm enough to winter the orange without protection.

Sidewalk trees: Locust and Mountain Ash [Locust and Acacia retinoides]. Interchange the two trees mentioned, plant sixteen feet apart and remove which ever kind proves the least acceptable as years pass by.

Arbor at entrance: Aristolochia and Scarlet Runners [Wistaria and Morning Glories].

Alongside of house: Stretch wire-netting against the house and train to it: Virginia Creeper, Clematis paniculata, Sweetwater Grape, Sweet Peas and Scarlet Runners [Akebia quinata, Tecoma grandiflora, Isabella Grape, Sweet Peas and Scarlet Runners]. Plant in the corner a Holly of the plain green-foliaged kind [Berberis Darwinii].

Near the animals train Flowering Quince against the wall.

Vines at the shelter: Wistaria or Japanese Morning Glories and Jasminum nudiflorum [Tecoma jasminoides and Lophospermum scandens].

Back of vegetable garden: Purple Hazel, Damson, Crabapple, and, along the street, Scarlet Peach. [Purple Hazel, Double Almond, Plumbago Capensis, and, along the street, Tecoma Capensis].

Arrange the vegetable garden to suit the kindergartner's ideas.

Along property-line on the south side: Quince or Medlar, Spiræa Thunbergii [Exochorda grandiflora], Forsythia Fortunei.

Along property-line on the west: Laburnum, Lilac, Snowberry, Colutea, Willow, Elder, Hawthorn, Briers, Heather [Purple Fringe, Philadelphus, Tamarix, Persimmon, Duckplant, Hawthorn, Willow, Briers, Diosma].

Bed beyond the arbor: Mulberries along the fence, Larch in the corner. Strawberries and Currants, etc.

Bed near the house (north side): Berries.

Perennial Border: Antirrhinum, Lamium, Bleeding Heart, Helleborus (in cold climates only), Forget-me-not, Sunflowers, herbaceous Spiræas (for cool places only), Gypsophyla, Columbines, Flags, Red Clover, Larkspurs.

Border along house: Pansies, Violas, Violets, Primroses, Pentstemon (clear colors only), Marguerites, Asters, Hollyhocks, Phlox, Hypericum.

Bulbous plants: Daffodils, Tigridias, Lilium album and tigrinum [pardalinum], Crown Imperials [Watsonias], Oxalis, Erythronium, Flags, Montbretias. At the house: Crocus, Snowdrops [Fairy Maids], Eranthis, Roman Hyacinths, Tritoma [Callas, Amaryllis Belladonna], Lilium longiflorum.

PLANTING OF A KINDERGARTEN ON A ONE-HUNDRED-FOOT LOT.

Refer to illustration on plate number seven. The north and the east side of the lot face the street.

Sidewalk trees: Set out, alternating, Birch and Poplar [Tulip-tree and Hawthorn] and remove in later years whichever kind gives the least satisfaction.

Arbor at east entrance: Weeping Laburnum or Elm.

Small bed next to arbor: Arundo Donax fol. var., Cannas, Tritoma, Gladiolus, Montbretias, Flags. Along barren space of fence train a Honeysuckle [an evergreen variety in warmer climate].

Plant Aralia, Ricinus and Elephant's Ear, underneath them Violets.

In triangle at corner of lot: Willow (training it against the fence in long branches), purple Hazel, Prunus Pissardii and Golden Currant. At this strip along fence train single Cherokee Rose or R. Wichuraiana. Rosa Rugosa and Briers in corner against arbor on north side. To form arbor, plant slit-leaved Birch, if Birches are along the sidewalk; otherwise, select Weeping Ash.

Back of toy-garden plot, along property-line plant: Spindle-tree, Soap-shrub, Golden Elder, Double Almond, Crab-apple, Colutea and Smoke-tree at corner where animals are housed. Against wall of house on next lot train flowering Quince and Boston Ivy [Ficus repens].

Along shelter and against house for animals train: Wistaria, Virginia Creeper and Hop-roots.

Vines and shrubs against house, beginning at corner of shelter: Jasminum nudiflorum, Riesling Grapevine, Cornel Cherry (at corner), Honeysuckle, Clematis and Scarlet Peach, Snowberries at the base. Little bed at front door: Magnolia Soulangeana and M. stellata, Xanthoceras [Plumbago Capensis]. Aristolochia, Tecoma grandiflora, Bridal-wreath, Pæonies, Barberries and Hypericums.

Horseshoe-bed surrounding swings fill with all varieties of Berries.

In the larger piece of lawn, ten feet from its edge, plant a Christmas Spruce opposite the seesaws and outer vegetable garden.

Perennial border: Nasturtium, Flags, Single Pæonies, Gladiolus, Lupinus and Lathyrus, Antirrhinum, Mimulus, Dead Nettle, Leonotus, Bleeding-heart, Larkspurs, Primroses, Daisies, Hepatica (not for warm positions), Forget-me-nots, Marguerites, Anemones, Gypsophilas, Hollyhocks, Phlox, Canterbury-bells, Carnations, Lychnis.

Bulbous plants: Every space and spot not planted otherwise may be filled in with bulbs.

The two large patches for vegetables admit of a varied display, and the wide strip from arbor on north side to the house for animals on the west side gives ample room for many little beds for toy-gardening. The division of these is a matter for the kindergartner to arrange.

Glancing over the designs, as herewith illustrated, we may well exclaim: A child raised in such surroundings can develop as cheerful as the bird in the bush, as free as the king of the desert, as perfect as the tree on a mountain meadow.

HIPS FROM A
WAY-SIDE BRIER.

Discrimination in what is to surround our children is worth volumes of teaching in later life.

————

Enlist things living to help you raise your child. A ball while active is, yet, a ball from day to day. How different a plant! Its slow but constant development, in bloom this week, in seed the next, addresses the child in every change.

————

The surroundings which we arrange about our kindergartens feed the mind, not the fancy. These gardens must offer the child an opportunity to develop. To look upon them primarily as a means for instruction is abusing their purpose and injuring the child.

————

The eye of a child is the mouth through which the brain-food enters. It is for you to determine what pictures may pass its absorbing vision.

————

Associate yourself with the best in the world, and you will have thousands of allies in your onward move. Oppose the good and every step you take will be a move backward.

Men are apt to err. A plant of nature tells its own story uninfluenced, unvarnished. Therefore, leave out those productions of cultivation which, like some fellow creatures, smack of overculture and insincerity.

Our first thoughts are true from within, our second influenced from without. So with our periods of life—the genuineness of childhood is natural, the complexity of later years is an artificial product.

The problem of a kindergarten is teaching through association; that of after years association through teaching.

What a strange age is this! We display our asylums and jails and hide away those few kindergartens which we suffer to vegetate.

To raise a child is to live life over.

The milk of love drawn through the nipple of common sense raises good kings, professors, and men-with-the-hoe.

Insight in a child's nature is to be the birthright of the kindergartner.

A masculine kindergartner—a goat for gardener.

There are two kindergartners who can succeed: the one because she has mastered all there is to be learned; the other because she has learned nothing.

A kindergartner—a sister of mercy of the holiest order.

The child is like the traveler in foreign lands: each day opens new continents to his vision, each day brings vast discoveries to him and not till after his return home does he sift his observations. So should a child not enter upon the age of thought till it has become accustomed to scenes and changes and can rest its mind in quiet meditation.

The merry brooklet as it passes dancing from rock to boulder, do you expect it to do more than furnish playground for the swift finny crowd, or a mirror for the golden faces of nodding flowers? Not till after it has gathered volume and settled down to a quiet stream do you think of harnessing its power, and using its element to wet the thirsty garden. So the child. Give it healthful play and joyful pastime, surrounded by the most cheering environment your mind can develop and your means can employ. As age adds to its strength and new fields are opening before it, it will become conscious of its enlarging abilities and seek employment to accomplish the best in the widest influence possible.

The smile of a child is a gleam from heaven.

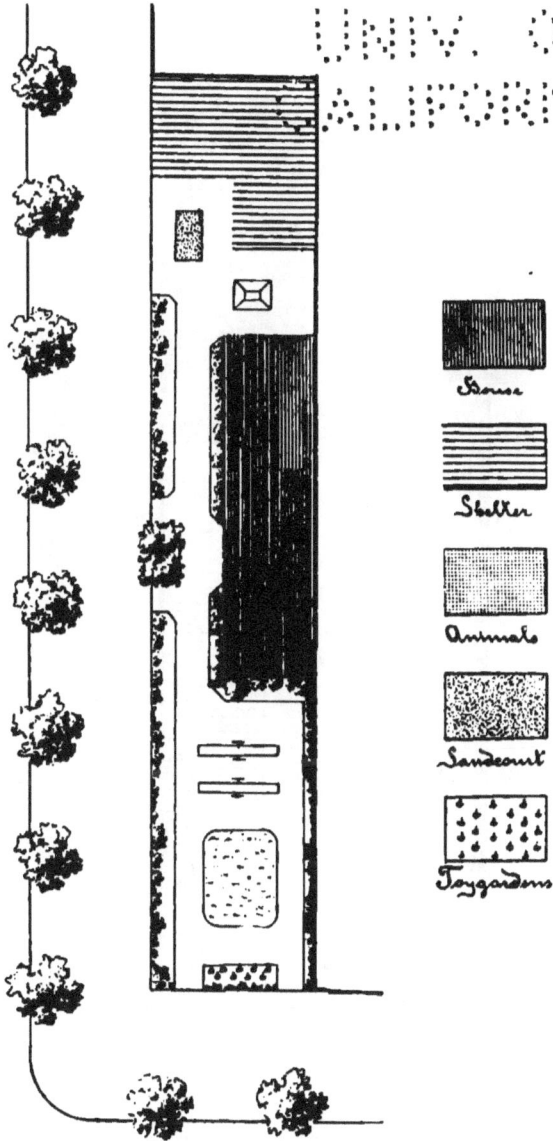

House

Shelter

Animals

Sandcourt

Toygardens

Plate No. 1

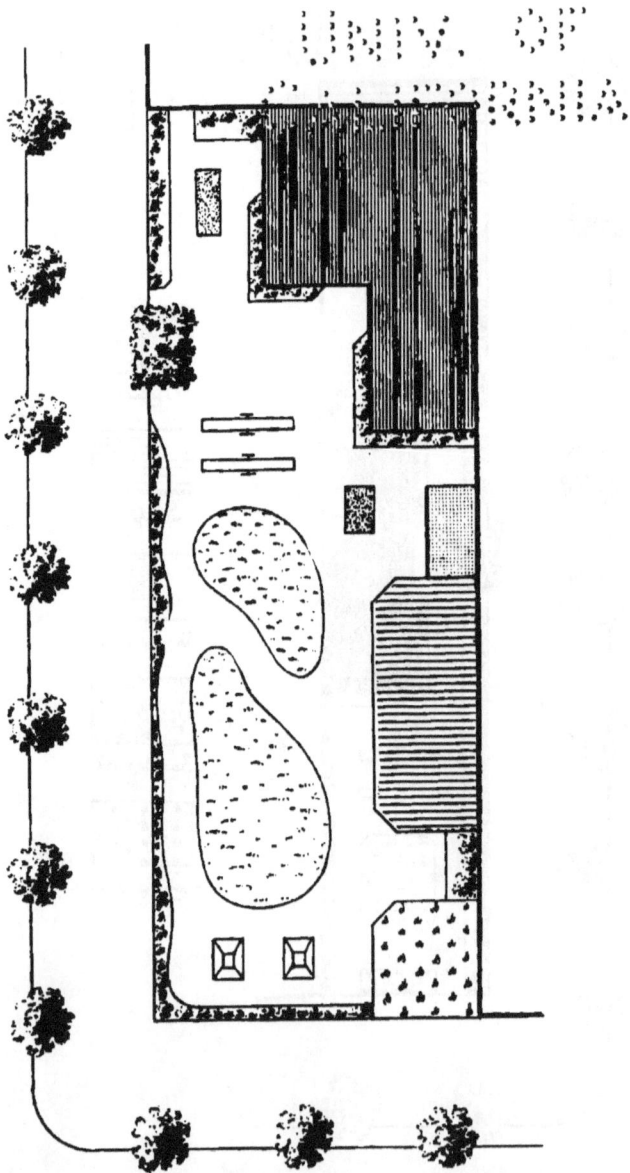

Plate No. 2

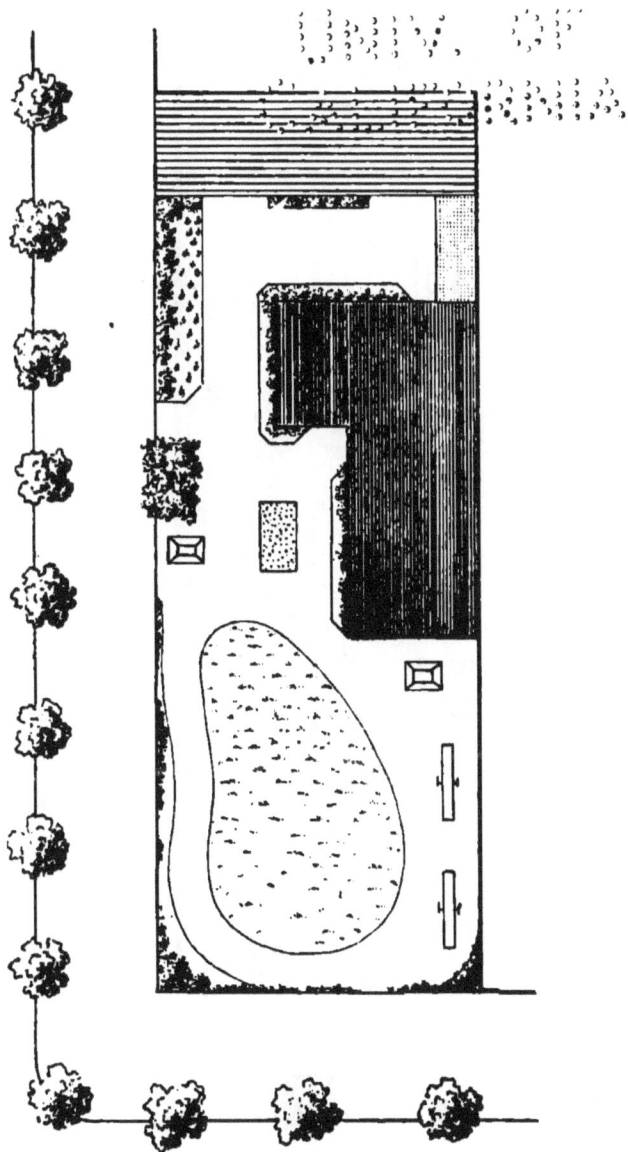

Plate No. 3

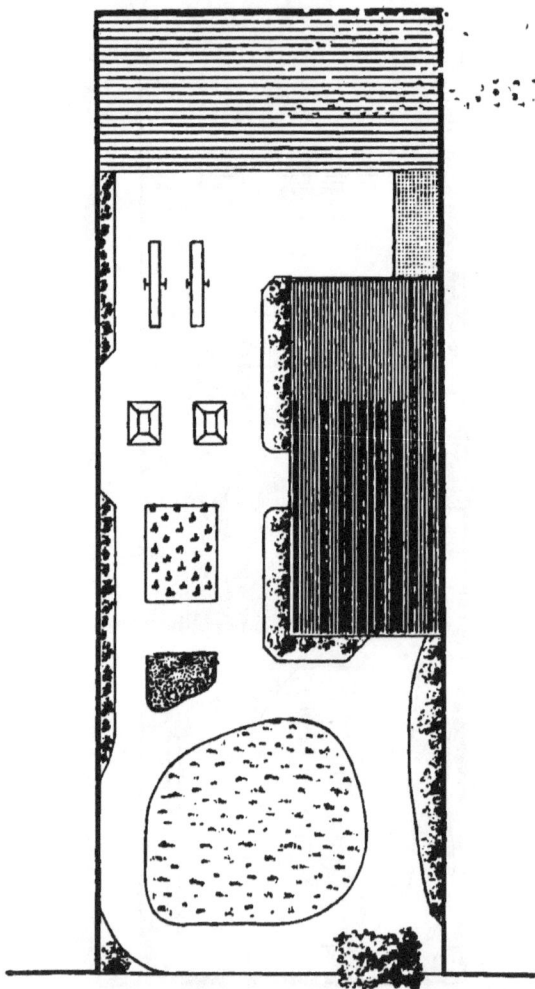

Plate No. 4

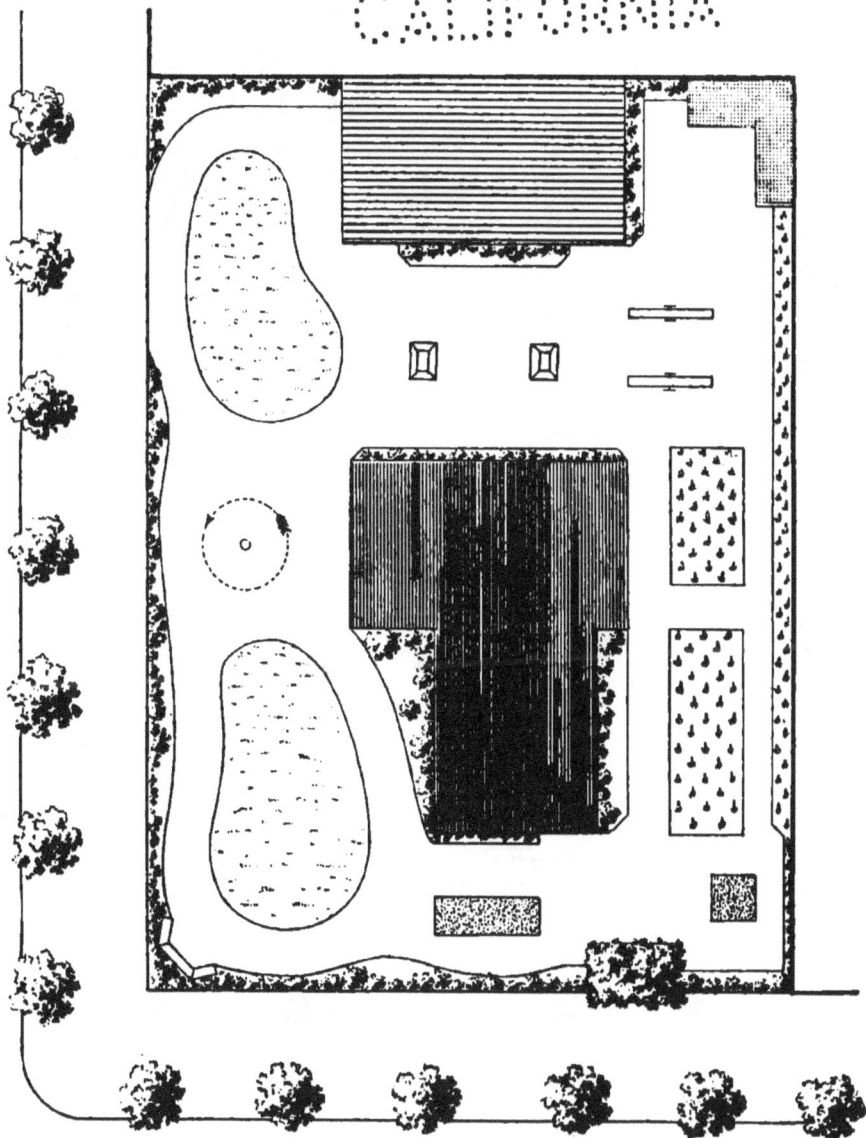

UNIV. OF CALIFORNIA

Plate No. 5

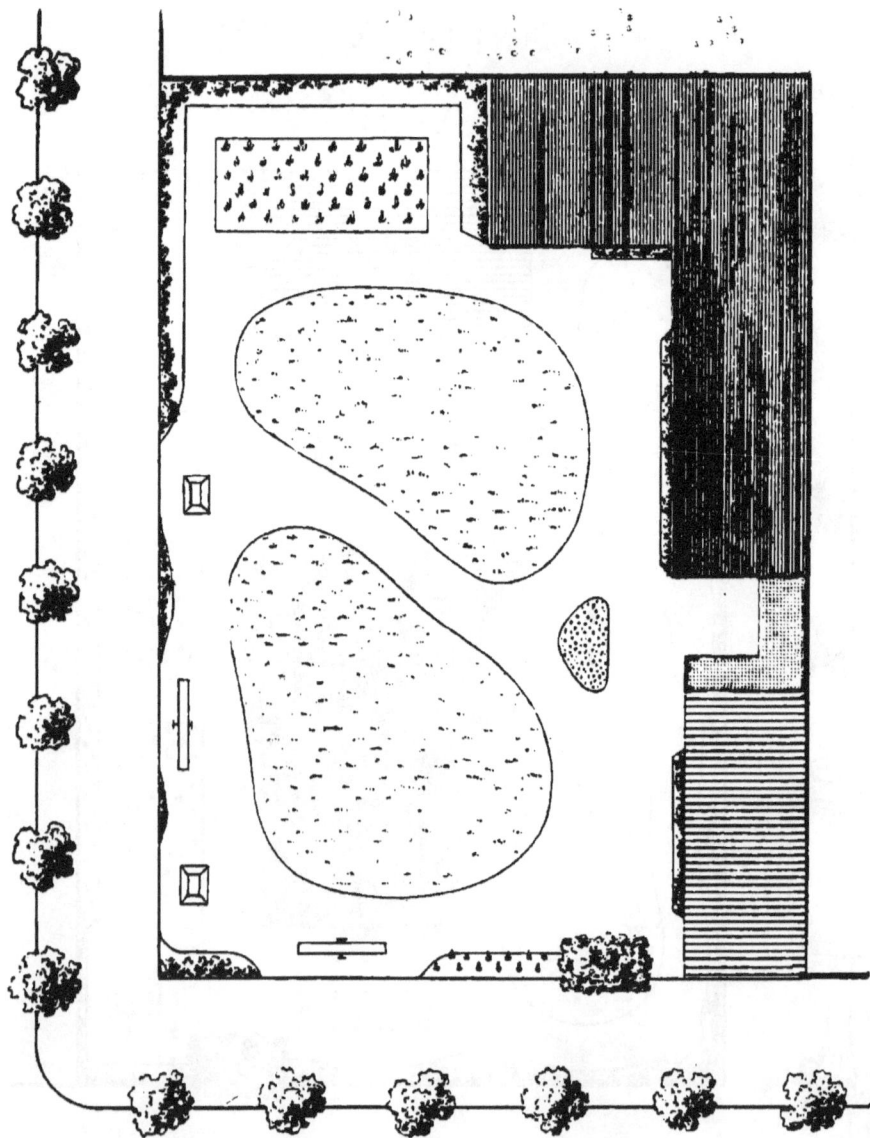

Plate No. 6

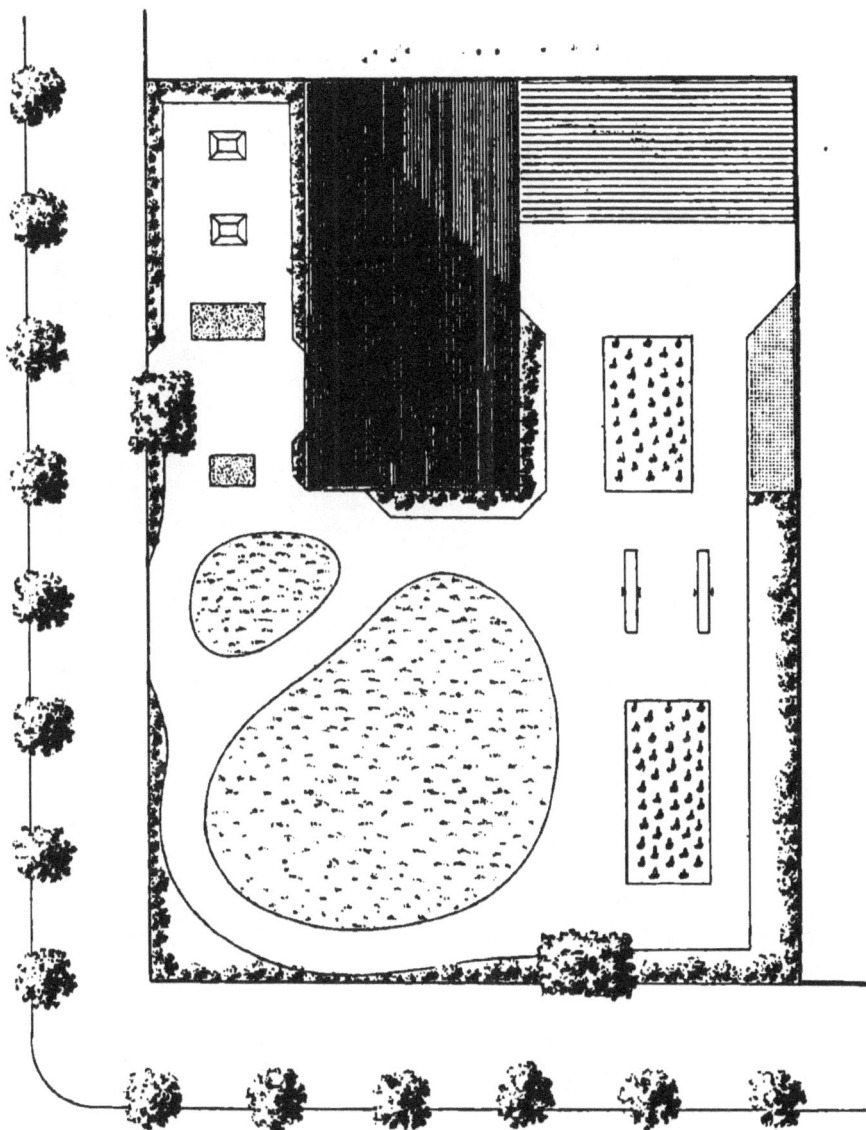

Plate No. 7

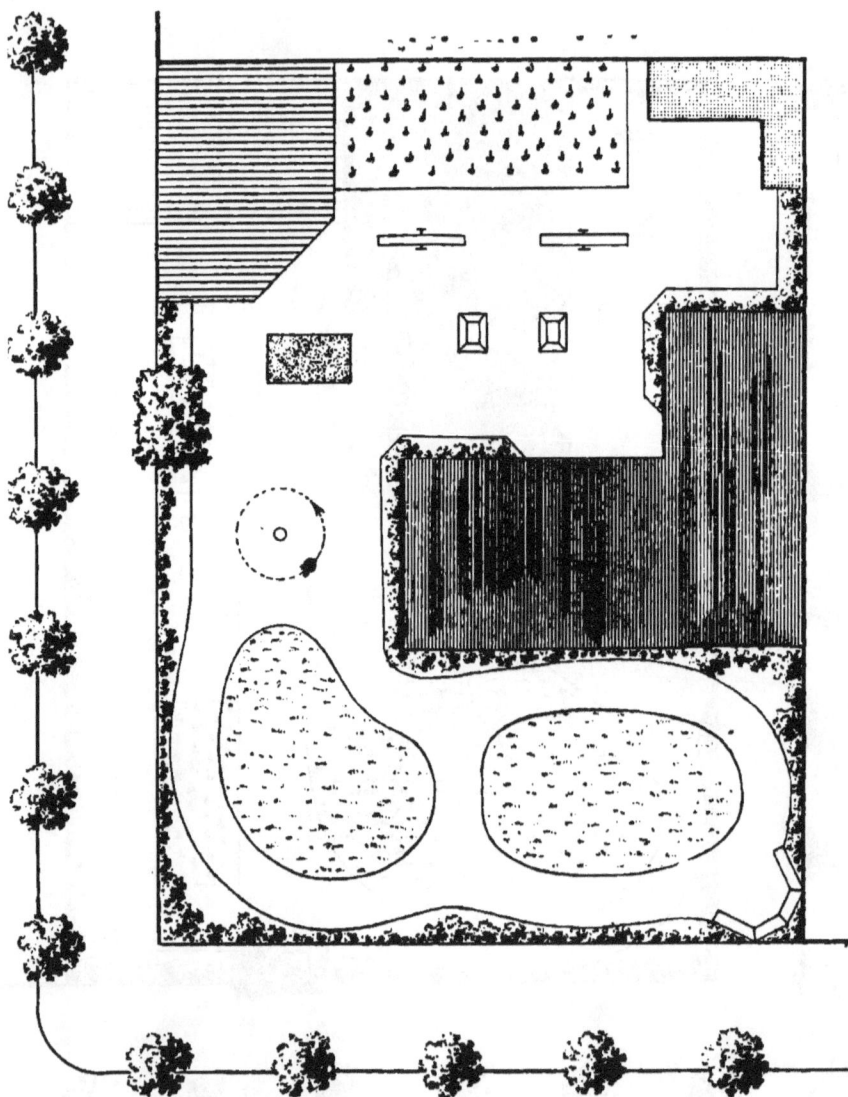

Plate No. 8

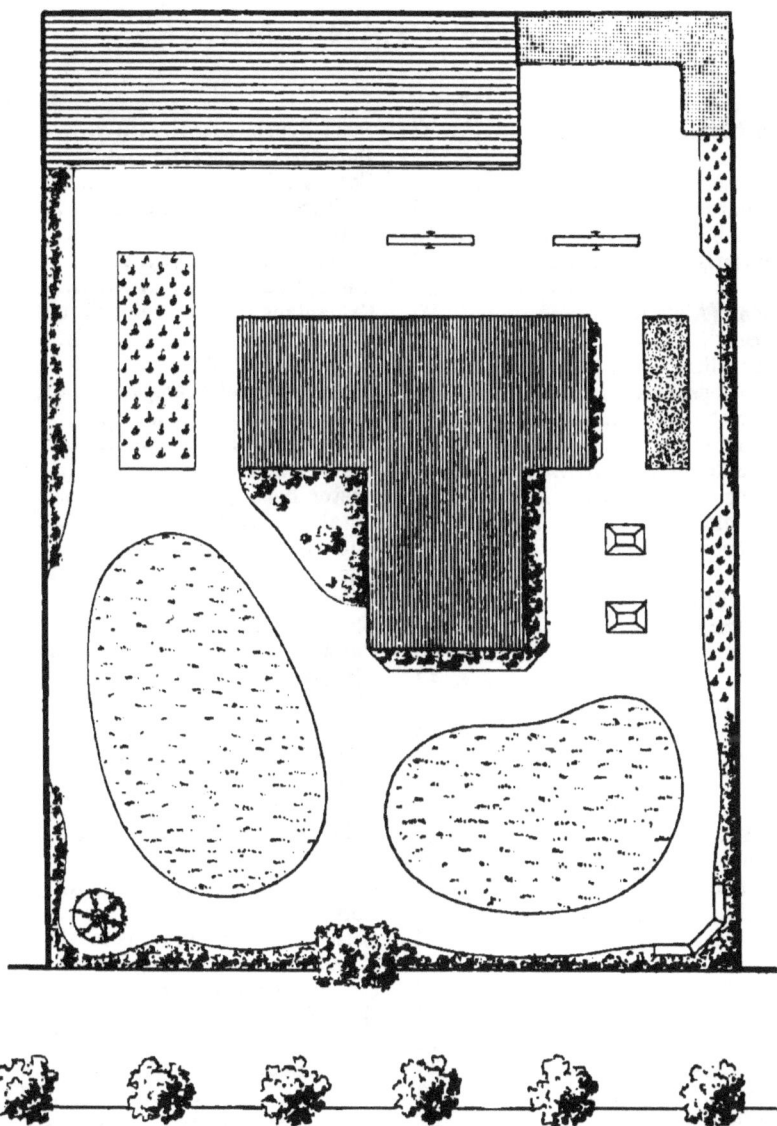

Plate No. 9

ÍNDEX OF PLANT NAMES.

74

www.ingramcontent.com/pod-product-compliance
Lightning Source LLC
Chambersburg PA
CBHW021525270326
41930CB00008B/1090